Praise for P

"While essential for beginners, the experienced jammer will also find invaluable information in this book. Follow the directions and improve both your musicianship and your manners!"
—Faith Petric, founder of the San Francisco Folk Music Club www.sffmc.org

" Playing well with others requires many important skills of listening, watching, and learning. This could take the average untutored player years to acquire... however Martha Haehl and Mike Walker have distilled all this wonderful knowledge into one collection that is in my opinion, a must read for all entry level and even intermediate players."
—Lil Rev, Milwaukee, World famous ukulele and blues harmonica entertainer (www.lilrev.com)

"Play Well With Others is a very good guide to help the beginning player learn how to play with other musicians and have the confidence to join in the fun. Give it a read and have many great jam sessions."
—"Country" Dave Harmonson, Seattle, professional musician since 1970

"Play Well With Others does a great job of addressing the issues that come up in jamming, with helpful suggestions and a sense of humor. I really enjoyed and recommend it."
—"Jumpin" Jim Beloff, Clinton, CT, Ukelele master and songwriter (www.fleamarketmusic.com)

"What a fun book! I never expected that a book on jamming would be such an entertaining read. Play Well With Others is full

of advice and instructions valuable to the beginning as well as the advanced jammer, plus just the right amount of music theory. It's chocked full of humorous insights. I would highly recommend it to anyone."
 —Susan Urban, Chicago Singer-Songwriter, member of *February Sky* www.februarysky.com

"Gosh, this is a concise guide on how to play music with others. You nailed the problem with noodlers between songs, folks not sensitive to the jam dynamic they are encountering, and the importance of letting the person who's leading stay in the forefront. With this book there is hope for the poor cartoonish Jack the jam buster character who learns throughout the book how to Play Well With Others."
 — Phil Cooper, Chicago, member of *February Sky*

"Play Well With Others is really friendly and nifty to be sure!"
 —Janet Klein, Alhambra, CA, renowned Tin Pan Alley singer and founder of *Janet Klein and her Parlor Boys*. (www.janetklein.com)

"Play Well With Others" is a great, much needed book for anyone who likes jam sessions. It's filled with information about music, but more importantly, it discusses the etiquette of jam sessions in a way that would make Miss Manners proud. You need this book!"
 —Dakota Dave Hull, professional guitar performer and recording artist. (www.dakotadavehull.com)

Play Well With Others

A Musician's Guide to Jamming Like a Pro

Martha Haehl   Mike Walker

How High The Moon Publishing
Kansas City, Missouri

Copyright 2009 © by Martha Haehl and Mike Walker. All rights reserved. No part of this publication may be reproduced, stored in a retrieval system, or transmitted in any form or by any means, electronic, mechanical, photocopying, recording, or otherwise without the prior written permission of the copyright holder, except brief quotations used in a review.

Editor: K.C. Compton
Illustrator: Jake Walker
Cover Design: Andy O'Hare

The purpose of this guide is to inform and entertain. The authors and How High The Moon Publishing shall have neither the liability nor responsibility to any person or entity with respect to any loss or damage caused, or alleged to be caused, directly or indirectly, by the information contained in this book.

Every effort has been made to make this guide as complete and accurate as possible. However, there may be mistakes, both typographical and in content. Therefore, this text should be used as general guide and not as the ultimate source of how to play music.

ISBN 978-0-9743606-3-8
LCCN: 2008930483
Copyright Permissions (see pgs 107-108)

Published by
How High The Moon Publishing LLC
9826 James A. Reed Rd.
Kansas City, MO 64134
Visit www.hhtmp.com for additional information.

Printed in the United States of America

This book is dedicated to anyone with the desire, dream or longing to make music with other people. We thank the countless jammers who keep grass roots music alive and continually inspire us to have fun while becoming better musicians.

Acknowledgements:

Thanks to Donna Costagin, Dave Harmonson, Karen Hendricks, Don Koke, Dave Lizor, Jamey Logan, David Ludwick, Nick Rivard, Loretta Rivard, Lynn Snyder, Steve Mason, Bob Smethers, Bob Suckiel, Diana Suckiel and Vicki Walker for all the help and suggestions in making this a better book.

Are you a jam buster? You can learn how to play well with others and be welcome at any jam!

You Need This Book If...

♪ You're an experienced jammer, but want to fine tune your skills and branch into other styles.

♪ You've always wanted to join a jam but, are terrified of the thought.

♪ When you join a jam, other musicians decide it's time for a snack.

♪ You're done playing when someone changes keys.

♪ You want to help friends learn how to play well with others.

♪ You'd love to know more about common chord progressions or music structure.

How To Use This Book

Part 1 covers jam do's and don'ts, and types and styles of jams. Whether you're a beginner or you've been playing for years, you need to know some basic rules of jamming, or you might become a *jam buster*. You can choose and pick the sections as you want or need, but we recommend reading the do's and don'ts before moving on.

Part 2 talks about things like music progressions, transposing, and musical keys, and gives you a musical foundation for jamming. Many a fine, experienced jammer plays by ear and does not intellectualize the structure of music. However, we think that a deeper

Play Well With Others

understanding of musical structure can help you play well with others.

Part 3 deals with the nuts and bolts of playing music, and serves as a basic music theory reference guide. Included are common chord progressions, a table of major chords and their relative minors, construction of major, minor and diminished chords and more.

Remember! The tips in this book are meant to help you have more fun in jams, not to scare you away from them. If you're in a jam that's really cookin' and you're having a great time, that's what really counts, even if your circle breaks a few jam rules. The authors do it all the time!

Also, if you are a veteran jammer, do everything you can to make that new jammer feel at home. Welcome novice jammers and help them improve their jamming skills.

Play Well With Others

Introduction

There's nothing more fun than making music with others…well, almost nothing. But if you don't know how to join in or haven't mastered the simple rules of etiquette when it comes to jamming, the fun turns quickly into frustration. That's why we start with do's and don'ts, jam types, and jam styles before we move to actual practice. No matter what level musician you are, do's and dont's is the one section not to be skipped!

Play Well with Others is written from a unique perspective. Co-authors Martha Haehl and Mike Walker come from opposite ends of the musical spectrum. Martha grew up playing and singing, and can play guitar, fiddle, and flute with the best of them. Even with that, she had to transition from reading notes on a page to listening and hearing the heart of a jam song.

Mike had never played until a chance encounter with a ukulele a few years ago. Martha brings her years of experience, while Mike can empathize with those just starting out because that's where he was not long ago.

Play Well With Others

We'll introduce common chord progressions from simple to complex. We'll help you understand them and have you try a few. We'll even get into the basics of transposing and how capos change keys, but not patterns. But it's more than that. ==To play well with others means knowing how to fit in, knowing when to do what, and knowing how to make sure everybody participates and has fun.==

Play Well with Others targets lead players, singers, and musicians who carry rhythm or provide structure by playing chords. The book doesn't have to be used sequentially. If you already know material in a section, just skip to a part you'd like to learn. (See? We're already teaching you to improvise!)

If you can count to four and listen, you are just a few steps away from being able to *Play Well With Others*. Read, practice, and most importantly, have fun jamming!

What is a Music Jam?

According to Wikipedia, a jam session is "a musical act where musicians gather and play without extensive preparation or pre-defined arrangements. Jam sessions are often used to develop new material, find suitable arrangements, or simply as a social gathering and communal practice session. Jam sessions may be based upon existing songs or forms, may be loosely based on an agreed chord

Introduction

progression or chart suggested by one participant, or may be wholly improvisational. Jam sessions can range from very loose gatherings of amateurs to sophisticated improvised recording sessions intended to be edited and released to the public."

Wikipedia adds that "Jam sessions are generally for the benefit of the performers and not part of a public performance."

Why Jam?

According to Don Koke, long time performer, jammer and owner of the Iron Horse Concert Hall in El Dorado, Kansas, "Jamming is one of the most satisfactory features of making music. It provides a gauge to measure one's musical knowledge and proficiency with little fear of overly exposing oneself as in a contest or recital. Jamming opens new musical vistas and challenges. Music is a window to the soul, and jamming allows one to share an intimate piece of oneself with others."

Jam Busters and Train Wrecks.

A jam buster is someone who breaks up the jam when the person starts to play. Other jammers hit the food table or pack up and go home. A train wreck is when a particular song falls apart. Throughout the book we'll present in cartoon form jam-busting examples and how to avoid or repair train wrecks. We like to think that most jam

Play Well With Others

busters are great people who are not intentionally busting up a jam but just need some tips for *Playing Well With Others*.

Jack the "Jam Buster"

Table of Contents

Introduction	11
Jamming Do's and Don'ts	17
From Head to Toe, Jam Anatomy!	29
Jam Types	33
Jam Your Genre	41
The Nitty Gritty of Jamming	49
Relative Minors	53
Easy Transposing	59
Capo and Capoese	63
A Circle That's Never Unbroken	67
Minor Keys	77
What Key Was That?	79
Take a Break, But Don't Lose Your Noodle.	81
Fakin' the Blues and the Beat Goes On	87
Nuts and Bolts	93

Play Well With Others

Does your instrument fit the music? Don't bring a trumpet to a dulcimer jam, a flute to a bluegrass jam, or an autoharp to a jazz jam.

Jamming Do's and Don'ts

"Don't bring a Trumpet to a Dulcimer Jam."
-Steve Mason

Jams come in wonderful varieties. Blend blueberries or strawberries with sugar and you have a tasty spread. For musical jams, take equal parts of instruments, songs, tunes, then add people and stir. The best jams are flavored with improvisation—making up and playing musical arrangements on the spot with other musicians.

Different jams may have different rules depending on the styles of music and the traditions of the people involved. When you join a new group, take a few minutes to observe and figure out how the jam works. Understanding the dynamics and using plain old common sense can greatly enhance the musical quality of a jam and make it a euphoric experience. Inexperienced musicians can participate too, and grow as musicians in the process.

Enjoy

Have fun! Relax and enjoy what happens. Don't make a job out of it. Forgive yourself and others for imperfect music. Recognize

Play Well With Others

and enjoy the perfect moments while celebrating the heart people put into music. The tips we provide are only guidelines. If you have a great jam going, don't mess with perfection. The important thing is that you're having fun and making good music.

Be Generous!

Take turns. You might go around in a circle and give everyone the option of picking or leading a song. Some of the best jams have a jam leader to keep things moving. Later you'll learn what makes a great jam leader.

In the spirit of sharing, help other musicians sound their best, even if the song they're playing is not your favorite. You might find out that the song turns out to be one of your favorites after all.

Tune

Tune your instrument to standard pitch. Unless you're one of the rare chosen people with perfect pitch, use an electronic tuner when available. An instrument that is in tune with itself may not be in tune with everybody else. If possible, tune somewhere else before joining a jam already in session. Don't tune in the middle of someone else's song! Instrumentalists who move capo positions or use different tunings for different keys may need time between songs to tune. Give them the time (and silence from music) to tune before the next song.

Jamming Do's and Don'ts

Make Artistic Judgements

Are you a flute player, fiddler, or musical saw player? If you play a dominating, potentially annoying lead instrument, just listen instead of playing during someone else's instrumental break or while someone is singing. At the very least lay back or compliment the lead by picking up frills at the end of phrases. It's easy to overshadow someone else's brilliant licks. When you lay out and then come back in, people will notice and enjoy it.

If you are the primary rhythm player, don't play lead unless someone else can pick up the rhythm. Solid rhythm is the heart and soul of good music, so if you are carrying the rhythm, then carry it.

Play in the Style of the Jam

The great country singer Roger Miller told us in song that "You can't roller skate in a buffalo herd." Likewise, you can't play your trumpet at a dulcimer jam, and *Michael, Row Your Boat Ashore* could get you thrown out of a swing or jazz jam.

When a song or tune is simple and lyrical, it deserves a simple, lyrical melody, so don't cram in 10 notes per second. Save that for a hot bluegrass tune. Blending with the group makes a jam fun.

In Between Songs

When the song is over, it's over, so quit already! It's hard to

Play Well With Others

start another song while some one is fiddling around on another tune so stop plucking around!

Sonic Space

The number of players in a jam affects what each player should play. The more players, the less each player needs to play. Individual orchestra members often play very little in a particular piece. In a trio, each player has more sonic space. If you are one of several guitar players in a jam, try to find something to do that is different from the others. Try playing voicings up the neck of the guitar, playing a chord on just the first beat of each measure, or sitting out on a whole verse or lead! Not playing is an underrated skill that makes an instrument all the more impressive when it comes back in.

During Songs

Attention singers: Enjoy those instrumental breaks and the occasional tune without words, and don't sing or talk through them. Likewise, if some other singer is leading the song, provide ornament. Harmonize on the chorus, add a little, not a lot every single time, no matter how well you sing.

Attention instrumentalists: If you're playing a rhythm instrument behind the singer, the operative word is *behind*. The singer needs to be front and center. If you're louder than the singer, pipe down! And don't over play your own singing.

Jamming Do's and Don'ts

Lead players: Silence can be golden. Don't play a lead part while the singer is singing. Sometimes the singer and back up rhythm players are the only ones that should be heard. Pauses and periods of silence are just as important as always playing.

Listen

This is the simplest, most challenging, and most important part. The person leading a particular song or tune controls the tempo and tone. Follow the leader. If you have to strain to hear the singer or lead player, you're playing too loud, so pipe down! Blending individual voices and instruments into an ensemble creates a beautiful song. Sometimes the eye is quicker than the ear, so keep good eye contact with the song leader and watch when he or she changes chords. You may know a wild, offbeat version of a song, but save your version for when you're the song leader.

Practice

If you want to lead a song, practice ahead of time and plan the song structure. Practice playing songs without stopping even if you make mistakes. Keep the beats easy and steady.

Have you ever dreamed of backing up Alison Krauss or Johnny Cash? If you have a radio or CD player, you can! Playing along with recorded music is a good way to learn. You have to stay with the beat of the recording because the recording is not going to adjust to you.

Play Well With Others

Put some thinking into the intro and outro. Like a junk yard dog sensing fear, jammers can sense if you're not confident about leading the song and they'll have a hard time following you, so play it like you mean it.

Don't Get Ticketed For Speeding

Playing tunes at breakneck speed often results in sloppy music and can leave other jammers choking in the dust. Slow down to feature the beauty of the music.

Driving Is Easier With a Map

If you're leading the song, call out the key of the song or tune you'll be playing and give jammers a heads-up about unusual curves ahead. Without warning signs, key or rhythm changes, weird chords, or a cappella breaks can throw the other jammers off course.

Leading a Song

When it's your turn to lead a song, don't panic or put the jam on pause while you sort through your mental musical database. If you don't have a song in mind, just pass your turn and try again the next time.

Pick a jammable song. Save your Mozart concerto for the Mozart jam. Remember to call out the key. You are the quarterback. Take note of the jam's musical level and pick something that fits in.

Jamming Do's and Don'ts

<u>Starting Off</u>

We love simple, and a simple way to start a song is to start strumming to set the beat. Then after a measure or two, start singing. If the group needs some help, play the song all the way through, singing the chord names to the melody instead of the words. If the song is a simple three-chorder, you might not need to teach the chords at all, unless you're playing in a beginner's jam.

A clever way to lead into a song is to play the last line. And for you followers, let the leader set the tone by waiting until after the intro to jump in.

<u>Give Me A Break!</u>

In most jams, there are at least a few people who play instrumental breaks. Where do you put in a break, how many do you insert, and how long does the break go? It all depends on the song. The instrumental or break usually happens at the verse or the chorus, or sometimes both. Often you'll be able to sense or feel when the time is right for a break. You might call out, "Take it, Martha," or "Take the break on the verse, Karen," or "Mike, pick it up on the chorus." If the other musicians get lost during the break, hum the melody to get everyone back on track.

Play Well With Others

Avoid giving too many breaks. An eight verse song doesn't need eight breaks, and some don't need any at all. Get to know the song you're leading, and you'll get a feel for the number of breaks and where they should go.

Jam groups have a life of their own, so observe. If players are yawning, checking grocery lists, or leaving a trail of drool, it's time to end the breaks, or maybe time to end the song. How do you do that?

It Ain't Over Till It's Over: How to End a Song

All good things must come to an end, including songs. In a Marx Brothers movie, Chico plays the same song chorus over and over again. While he drives everybody crazy, he explains that he can't think of the finish. Groucho says he can't think of anything else.

Once, during a jam, Mike began playing *Shine on Harvest Moon*. After about a dozen verses and instrumentals, he just kept on playing. Why? He didn't know how to end it! Mercifully, Martha musically communicated on her violin that the song was OVER, or else we would still be playing instead of writing.

How do you signal that you're wrapping it up? Ending a song is simple if you know how.

An easy way is to repeat the last line of a song once or twice. "Heads up for a turnaround" or "tag it", means "lets play the last

Jamming Do's and Don'ts

line one more time and end it." If somebody raises his or her foot up, don't flinch. That's another end-of-song signal. A very popular way is to holler out "one more time!" or "Let's take it on home."

When You're Not Playing

When you're grabbing a snack or drink, or if you came with friends just to listen, you are no longer a jammer, but part of an audience, and the audience has do's or don'ts, too. If the jam is the main event, let the musicians jam. If you choose to come and listen, then listen! Don't sit in the circle or at the edge and carry on conversation or laugh loudly at somebody's joke during a song. Musicians are a lot like golfers. It's all about the music! It's a jam, already! However, if jamming is one of several events at a picnic or potluck, the jammers may need to find their own space away from the conversation or other activities.

Bringing Your Band to a Jam

When your established band joins a jam, beware of inadvertently cutting other musicians out. Open up your arrangements to lead players and other singers. That way, you stretch your vision of a song while other jammers benefit by playing along with your well-structured music. Don't turn the jam into your band's performance; play along with selections by other musicians.

Play Well With Others

<u>Singing Along</u>

When singing along, follow! Some of the lyrics or phrasing may be different from what you know, so listen carefully and adjust. For example, if the lead singer is trailing off at the ends of lines, you should also trail off. If the singer is putting in some syncopation that you don't usually put in, then try to match it. Listen harder than you sing and watch the lead singer's lips. Lead singers, follow the beat and sing confidently so that people can sing along! With that said, not everything is a sing along. Listen to and appreciate those really great solos.

***

Jams would be so much easier, but not nearly as much fun, if there were just one generic jam type or style. But the types and styles are many, and what is acceptable in one will get you thrown out of another. The next two sections talk about different jams styles and types. It's so much better to get a boot out of a jam than to get booted out of one.

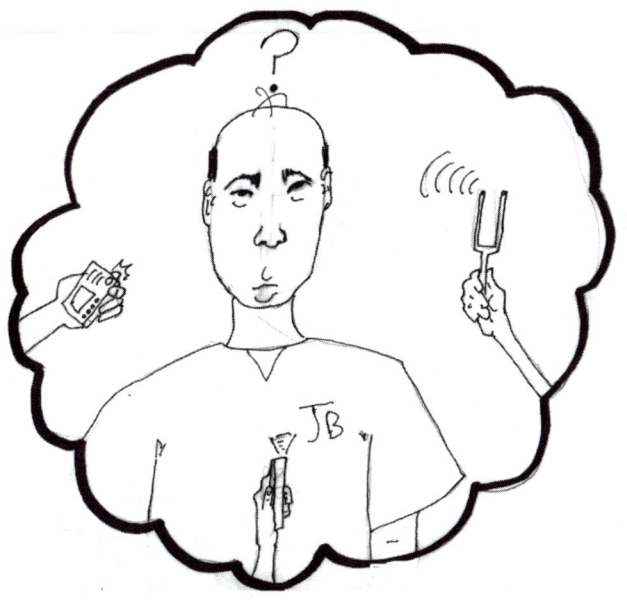

Stay in tune! Tuners are like mints, if someone offers you one, use it!

Play Well With Others

From Head to Toe, Jam Anatomy!

Wow! It's working! You can play along with tons of songs and fit right in. But what if you're sitting in the jam circle and suddenly it's your turn to pick a song and lead? Easy? It can be, if you know how to do it. Let's review some jamming tips.

Add variety to the jam by picking a song in a different key from the last one. If the song you're thinking about is too similar to the one just played, wait a few songs to play it.

Here are some simple suggestions for starting a song:

♪ Solidly strum the tonic chord in rhythm to set the tone of the song. Then start singing.

♪ Play through the chords of the last line of the song. Even better, practice ahead with another musician so that the melody of the last line of the song is played along with the chords.

♪ If you need to teach the chords, sing the chords to the melody while playing through the entire form of the song. Be careful with this one, however, if the musicians in the group can pick up chords on the fly, don't bore them to tears by tediously going through the

Play Well With Others

three chords of a song. You might instead give a heads up about anything out of the ordinary in the structure. For example, "It goes to F# on the bridge."

How many instrumental breaks should a song have and who should play them? Those are tough calls. If you have a lot of lead players, not everyone should get a piece of every tune, so take turns, not only within a tune but over the course of several songs or tunes.

It is important to signal breaks. Don't just stop singing and expect the instrumentalists to know who should play a lead. Either with a verbal cue, eye contact or a nod, signal who should play and on what part—the verse, the chorus, or both. You might plan leads before a song is started by asking who "wants a piece of this one?" Most importantly, be sensitive to the music. Some songs warrant multiple breaks while others don't need any.

So what if the tune is falling apart on an instrumental break? This happens for many reasons.

    1. Some players are on the chorus while some are on the verse.

    2. The lead player started earlier or later than the other musicians.

    3. The lead player doesn't have the tune committed to memory.

For whatever reason, if musicians are lost, as leader, start humming

Jam Anatomy

the melody where you think the song should be and bring the song back together. If you're one of the lost musicians, follow the leader. In such a situation, it is not a bad idea to shorten the break and go back to singing.

Wrapping It Up

You can start songs by strumming the first chord to set the rhythm, or you might sing through the song, singing the chords to the melody. Take turns giving breaks and plan them. If musicians get lost, hum the melody or start singing a new verse. Likewise, don't just quit at the end of a song, plan the end and give cues when the song or tune is ending.

***

Train Wreck: The rhythm is off.

Get Back On Track: Play softer or drop out entirely while the leader takes charge. Even if the leader of the song is off or has an erratic rhythm, a solid bass player in tandem with a rhythm guitarist might be able to pull the song back together. This is not the time for fancy picking. Defer to the best rhythm guitarist in the jam.

Play Well With Others

Jam Types

To participate in a jam (musical) without creating a jam (mess), it's important to know whether the jam is large or small, beginner or advanced.

Slow Jams

Slow jams help beginners learn how to play spontaneously with other jammers. Stick to simple three-or four-chord songs. Some three or four chorders are the most beautiful songs ever written, with a simple, innate beauty. Neither the songs nor the musical arrangements need to be boring.

Musicians or jammers should prepare for a jam by practicing lyrics and chords ahead of time. Learn the song well enough to play it all the way through. Concentrate on how the other musicians are playing instead of staying glued to the music in front of you. As long as you're staring at the music you're not really jamming, so learn the song, already! Pick a simple song with a steady beat and no more than four chords.

Play Well With Others

You're not Bruce Springsteen (if you're reading this, Bruce, sorry—and thanks!) So rather than trying to imitate your favorite musician (usually badly), focus on keeping a steady, solid beat. Easy does it! Avoid the common mistake of confusing "hard-driving" energy with "faster and louder." That's a real jam busting trap. Concentrate on style and expression.

Blend in with the rhythm and feel of the music. If you are unsure of the chords, play along, but very softly. If you can't hear the song leader, pipe down. If the song leader is playing too softly, encourage the leader to play and sing louder.

If you're leading a song, play and sing confidently. Focus on the song's meaning and keep the rhythm steady. That's a tall order, but with practice you can do it.

Leading a Slow Jam

Musical magic can happen in a slow jam when there's an experienced musician to lead the way. If that's you, here are some guidelines:

1. Teach musicians to play well with others. For example, give suggestions on how to stay together. If the lead singer or rhythm guitarist is being drowned out, stop the song if you have to and remind the other musicians to lay back. Or if the problem is a shy

Jam Types

lead musician, encourage him or her to play and sing more confidently. If there's a train wreck or the song is falling apart, just stop the song and start over. Help beginners learn to listen and play well with others.

2. Start with simple three-chord songs in major keys and progress to minor keys and more chords as you feel the group can handle it.

3. Participants might bring song sheets to share. That's okay, but wean them off the sheets so they can learn to play well with others by listening to the music.

4. To teach a song to the group, sing the chords to the melody before starting a song and singing the lyrics. If a song is at the higher end of the group's capability, try going through the song slowly at first, then bring the song up to speed.

5. Help beginners develop a sense of keys by playing the same song in more than one key.

6. Put on the brakes if the group starts playing different beats or rhythms. Remind the group to listen to each other, then start again. Even if you're the only lead player, add instrumental breaks to teach beginning musicians how to make space for them.

Play Well With Others

Mixed Skill Level Jams

When there's a mix of skill levels in jams, the experienced jammer should not expect every song to have a complicated structure, so respect others and pick songs within reach of other musicians. Likewise, the less experienced jammer may need to sit out or lay back on some of the tunes. Jams tend to trend towards the level of the least skilled musician. To keep a mixed skill jam from morphing into a slow jam, beginners should play softly or sit out on songs above their skill level.

Advanced Jams

The real excitement of jamming comes from playing with other musicians who challenge you to raise your playing level. Playing with musicians at a higher level than you helps you improve your technique, learn riffs, and branch into new musical styles. You become a better musician on the spot. However, don't bring those great musicians down to the lowest common denominator by playing too loudly, off beat, or out of the style of the song.

Feeling a little intimidated? That's normal and OK. Play quietly at first. There are no rules against just listening part of the time. Keep a keen ear out for what makes the music you love great and how the great jammers blend the music and share the spotlight. Pay

Jam Types

attention to how they phrase lyrics and instrumental breaks, or how they compliment the singer or lead player.

Large Jams

Corralling 10 fiddlers, 30 singers, 8 banjo players, 4 mandolin pickers, and 16 guitarists can be like herding cats. Somebody should be the DSB (Designated Song Boss).

DSB, here are your instructions: Pick songs familiar to most people or songs that are easily learned, not some fifth century Byzantine chant. Call and response lines and repetitive choruses are fun. Call on song/tune leaders who play and sing confidently.

Have instrumentalists share the breaks. For example, have all the fiddlers play during a break, or feature everyone wearing a tall hat. On occasion, showcase a particular musician who is exceptionally good.

Why not just split into smaller jams? Many times that is a good idea, if possible. However, at one of Martha's favorite annual events, the Walnut Valley Festival, many a fiddler or picker looks forward to playing synchronous tunes (mostly Celtic) with 20 to 100 other musicians under a mega tent at Carp Camp. This is not the typical jam. Many of the hard-core Carp Campers practice tunes in advance that are posted on a web site and come to Winfield knowing standard

Play Well With Others

fiddle tunes as well as newly composed tunes. In such a jam, don't expect the DSB to pick only songs that middle of the road players know or can pick up quickly. If you are learning tunes, stay on the fringes and play softly.

***

Wrapping It Up

Some really talented musicians don't play well with others because they never learned the do's and don'ts. Follow these tips and regardless of your skill level, you'll be welcome at almost any jam.

***

Train Wreck: You're playing in a different style than everyone else.
Get Back On Track: Back off, listen, and blend in.

Jam Types

When to Join a Jam

For Martha, the September Walnut Valley Festival in Winfield, Kansas is a must. People pour in from all over the world to hear some of the world's best acoustic musicians, but what she really loves is the parking lot jams that earned the festival its subtitle—Picker's Paradise.

Hundreds of jams may be going on simultaneously, all day and all night. One jam might be bluegrass, another swing, another old fifties rock 'n' roll, and yet another Celtic. You never know what you'll stumble into.

When you approach a circle of jammers, do you join, and how do you join? The best bet is to wait to be invited or ask, "Is it alright if I play along?"

Don't be offended if a jam isn't open. Sometimes pickers are sharing new or old songs with friends they only see once a year, or they might be preparing for contests. You might have run across a band rehearsing for a performance.

Once you join the jam, don't try to commandeer the jam to your rules or tastes.

Play Well With Others

Don't talk to musicians during songs!

Jam Your Genre

You've practiced and practiced, your blues songs are ready to go and you hear about a jam downtown. You walk into the jam room only to find a plethora of fiddles playing what sounds like Irish jigs. Bring your blues styles to a Celtic jam and you'll be in a bigger jam than you thought.

Beware your first pluck!

When you're a stranger to a new jam, lay back for a while, and check out the genre and dynamics of the group. Jams often have unstated rules depending on the group, or even the region, so ask a regular about how things go. Some groups may not appreciate your really innovative arrangement, clever political diatribes, or social or religious commentaries.

Once you've figured out the style and tone, adapt to it and don't try to make the jam adapt to you. Those stoic banjo players just might use that heavy metal rim and hardwood resonator for some-

Play Well With Others

thing besides playing. Your electric instrument or saxophone might be perfect for swing or country, but won't work in a Celtic jam.

Let's take a look at the characteristics of different jam styles.

Bluegrass is not exactly folk, swing or country, but elements of all are present. Be aware of which instruments are acceptable in the group you want to join. Traditionally, bluegrass instruments are fiddle, banjo, guitar, stand-up bass, mandolin, and dobro, all acoustic.

Other stringed instruments may or may not be welcome. Harmonicas are the most likely acceptable non-stringed instruments, with bones and spoons a close second. However, some bluegrassers consider bones and spoons taboo, possibly because they've encountered bones and spoons players who can't keep rhythm or who play too loudly or too much.

To hear the defining sounds of bluegrass, listen to Bill Monroe and the Bluegrass Boys. Bill Monroe literally invented the genre. Lester Flatt and Earl Scruggs further defined the hard-driving finger-picking bluegrass banjo sound.

Contrary to common opinion, the majority of bluegrass music is moderate or slow. Fast does not equal bluegrass. Tight upbeats and downbeats with the lead players cranking out sixteenth notes—16

Jam Your Genre

notes over a two beat (down-up, down-up) pulse—are typical of bluegrass music. Add the high lonesome tight vocal harmonies, crisply delivered, and you've got the best of bluegrass. Plenty of bluegrass songs are three-chorders, but don't underestimate the genre. Picking a hot lead, playing rhythm guitar/mandolin, or singing bluegrass style takes practice and skill. Listen carefully, do your best to blend in, and you will get it down.

Percussion, particularly tambourine or drums, is barely tolerated (if at all) by many bluegrassers. Tread carefully, and if no one throws a banjo at you or gets up and leaves every time you get your tambourine out, you are probably playing minimally—adding just a few tasty fill-ins.

In bluegrass music, lead players take turns and improvise lead parts around the form of the song. This is a surprising connection between bluegrass and jazz, where lead players also take turns and improvise around the form of the song. In contrast, in Celtic music, lead players play the melody, period.

Celtic music draws its roots from the Celtic people of Western Europe. To jump in on a Celtic tune, musicians need to be able to sight read, know the tune in advance or pick up tunes really quickly. Playing fiddle tunes in unison is the rule, and harmonizing or improvising is rare.

Play Well With Others

Excitement builds when instruments come in one at a time. Concertinas, accordions, fiddles, wooden flutes, tin whistles, and mandolins are a perfect fit for the Celtic style, as are guitars, tenor banjos, and banjos (played in a frailing style). The bodhran, a Celtic hand-held drum, is the percussion instrument of choice. As with any style, playing off-rhythm or too loudly can totally ruin the music. Celtic singing is usually solo or sometimes in unison.

Harmony Singing is all about the singing, and instruments are played minimally, mostly for rhythm. You might be the greatest lead player in the world, but you probably won't be called on to play a lead. Don't take it personally. Singing is the heart of this type of jam and singers are there to raise their voices, not play solitaire while listening to somebody improvise. Many songs are sung a cappella. That means stop playing!

Old-Time Fiddle Tune jams feature folk or contra dance tunes. Ukuleles, autoharps, dulcimers, or flutes might sneak in along with bones and spoons, but the most common old-time instruments are the fiddle (surprise!), guitar, mandolin, stand-up bass, and the banjo, usually played in a claw hammer or frailing style.

Often in old time fiddle jams every musician plays all the way through every tune. Sometimes instrument groups like mandolins

Jam Your Genre

are featured one time through the tune. As with bluegrass, a lot of fiddle tunes have just three or four chords. That doesn't mean that learning to play back up behind fiddle tunes is a slam dunk. It takes practice to hear when the chords change, especially in fast moving tunes, and to play rhythm that matches the style.

Good luck trying to change keys of a fiddle tune because keys are often set in stone. If you're emulating Michelle Shocked in your performance of a standard tune, go for the creativity. It's your show. In a jam, however, whether you're in Kentucky, Missouri, or New York, *Soldier's Joy* is played in the key of D while *Red Haired Boy* and *Old Joe Clark* are in A, all played at a fast clip. *Beaumont Rag* is played in F with a ragtime or swing beat. Got it?

In Jazz or Swing Jams the lead instrumentalist typically plays the tune all the way through, followed by another lead player doing the same. Instrumentalists sometimes share the breaks by trading "fours" or "eights." That means two or more instrumentalists trade off every four or eight measures.

Let a jazz singer solo and embellish the song. Don't add harmonies. Sometimes jazz singers sing duets, but those usually require advance practice. Even if you are the next Ella or Satchmo, let the singer solo and wait your turn. Instrumentalists should take turns picking up ends or playing riffs around the singer or lead player.

Mixed Genre jams are so much fun because there is something for everybody. Depending on the jam, bluegrass, Celtic, swing, or rock 'n' roll are all possible. Johnny Cash sandwiched in between Count Basie and Peter, Paul and Mary? That's OK! If you're not familiar with a song style, either play very quietly or don't play at all. Listen and enjoy!

Turning On The Juice—Electric Jams

So far we've talked about acoustic jams. What happens when we plug in? Country music and jazz jams are often the electric kind, and naturally the rules are different.

Electric jams, whether country or jazz, get cluttered when there are too many instruments, so musicians rotate in and out. Often a core of musicians play and invite a fiddler, horn player or pedal steel player, singer or bassist, to sit in for a song or two. Most often, you'll do more listening than playing.

Electric instrumentalists beware! You can blast out the room if you want to, so know when to play loud and when to back off.

Enough with just reading! The rest of the book chapters are hands-on, so get warmed up and ready to work and have fun!

***

Jam Your Genre

Playing the Right Instrument in the Style of the Music

Martha first got interested in folk music through open stages where Peter, Paul and Mary music and traditional folk songs were the norm. When Martha attended a bluegrass festival she got some really strange looks and could break up a jam quickly when she walked up with a flute. Being a quick study however, she put the flute in the case, listened carefully to the bluegrass rhythms and harmonies and began learning to play rhythm guitar and to sing vocals to a really exciting style of music.

Play Well With Others

Don't waste time plowing through your music when it's your turn to lead. Be ready when it's your turn, or pass until the next time around.

The Nitty Gritty of Jamming
Oh Say Can You "C"?

If you can read music, you're one step ahead in the game. But even if you don't read music you can still understand what keys are and how chords form songs.

Remember how formulas worked in algebra? Been trying to forget? Well, formulas have a role in music, with patterns in one key showing up in the others. We are going to start out with patterns in the key of C. And just for the heck of it, let's assign a Roman numeral to each note, starting with C as I.

I'm not a Harvard grad, but that would make D the number II and E the number III. F would be IV and G gets to be V. Get it? That's a switch from algebra, where letters stand for numbers! The notes, C-D-E-F-G-A-B-C are the I-II-III-IV-V-VI-VII-VIII of the C Scale.

Play Well With Others

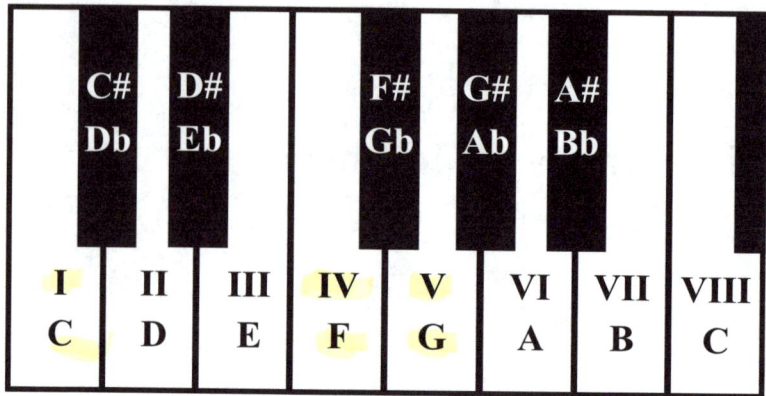

Guitarists or fiddlers might wonder why we're starting with a graphic of a keyboard. Well, it's a great visual for understanding the layout of music, even if you are not a pianist. We chose the key of C because all the notes are white keys, no sharps or flats.

Many songs are structured around the I, IV and V chords, which in the key of C are C, F and G, with the first, fourth and fifth notes of the C Scale as their roots. Such songs are sometimes referred to as "simple three-chorders." Below is the chorus of *Amazing Grace* along with the chords in the key of C.

```
         C                F           C                      G
Amazing Grace, how sweet the sound that saved a wretch like me
         C                F           C                 G   C
I once was lost, but now I'm found, was blind, but now I see.
```

How will this help you jam? You won't believe how many three-chorders there are. *Camptown Races, Oh, Susanna, Red River Valley* and many other common songs are built around the I-IV-V chords.

The Nitty Gritty of Jamming

***

You Practice: Play the chords C, F, G until you'll remember that the main chords used in the key of C are C, F, and G. Those three chords can come in any order, like:

F-G-C-F-G-C

C-G-C-G-C

C-G-C-G-C-F-G-C

Listen to the variations and try to spot them in songs.

Here's a term we'll use a lot: *progression.* A progression is a sequence or pattern of chords. Congratulations! You just practiced several progressions in the key of C using C, F and G.

***

Want to spiff your song up a little? In *Amazing Grace*, instead of moving straight from C to F, throw a C7 in between. Then make the last G in each line a G7.

C C7	F	C	G7

Amazing Grace, how sweet the sound that saved a wretch like me

C C7	F	C	G7 C

I once was lost, but now I'm found, was blind, but now I see.

Play Well With Others

A chord is made up of several notes played simultaneously. To form a major chord, start on the first note of a major musical scale, play the first note, skip a note and repeat this pattern until you have three notes. You just formed the I chord (or tonic chord) made up of the I, III, and V notes of the scale. So, in the key of C, the tonic chord C is C-E-G. The F chord is F-A-C, and the G chord is G-B-D.

***

Wrapping It Up

To make a chord into a seventh, add the seventh note of the scale, but take it down one-half step. That's called flatting the seventh. B is the seventh note in the C scale, so to make a C7, play a C chord plus the B*b* note. That's C-E-G-B*b*. F# is the 7th note of a G scale, so G7 is G-B-D-F.

The I, IV and V chords in a key are all you need to play a lot of songs. Vary the order and add in some seventh chords and it is amazing how many simple melodies you can make.

Relative Minors: Why Don't You Doo-wop, Like Some Other Folks Do?

Relative Minors: We're not talking about your bratty 12 year old nephew. A relative minor is a minor chord that starts on the 6th note of the related major scale. Stay with us: It's not complicated, just new.

The big question is: Who Cares about relative minors? The answer: We do! Why? Because once you add the relative minor to those three-chord songs, you'll be able to play a ton of the great songs of the Fifties, and more.

How do you figure out what the relative minor is? Well, it's time to introduce a tool, called a Circle of Fifths, as a quick and dirty way to pick out the relative minor (well, maybe not dirty if you wipe the guacamole off your circle kit found in the back of the book).

In the diagram on the next page, each major chord on the outside of the circle is paired with its relative minor. Finding relative minors this way is a lot easier than the ID tags, fingerprinting, or

DNA samples you might have to do for your other relative minors! If you have your Circle of Fifths wheel handy, rotate the inside circle so that the A on the inside aligns with the C on the outside. Make the inside chords minors, then they are the relative minors to the outside major chords. Later in the book you'll find an entire chapter on the Circle of Fifths as a tool to identify common chord progressions and transpose keys.

Circle of Fifths
Major Chords (Outside) & Relative Minors (Inside)

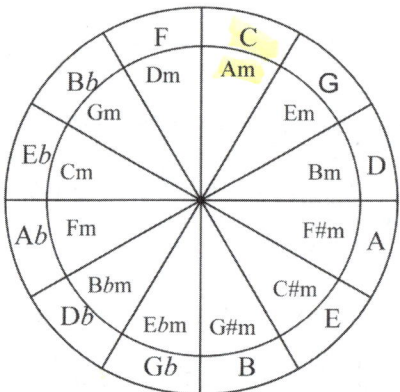

Doo-wop music gets a lot of mileage with progressions that blend relative minors in with a I-IV-V progression. The relative minor for a C chord is A minor, or Am. The relative minors for the IV and V chords in a key might also sneak into a tune. In the key of C, the IV and V chords and their relative minors are F (Dm) and G (Em).

Relative Minors

Learn the progression, C-Am-F-G and you'll be playing doo-wop songs in a heart (and soul) beat. See how nicely the progression works with *Blue Moon*.

```
     C   Am  F            G        C   Am    F
Blue moon,          you saw me standing alone

     G         C   Am  F         G            C
Without a dream in my heart    without a love of my own.
```

Besides giving doo-wop music its distinctive sound, relative minors make for really nice transitions. *Good Night Irene*, for example, can be played as a three-chord song, but adding a relative minor really adds the soy sauce to your chow mein.

***

You Practice: Practice the C-Am-F-G progression until you really get the feel for it, then try it with *Blue Moon*. Then play *Good Night Irene,* first without the relative minor (continue playing an F), then with, and listen to the difference.

```
    C        G             C
Irene good night, Irene good night

            C7        F    Dm
Good night, Irene, good night, Irene,

     G              C
I'll see you in my  dreams.
```

Play Well With Others

Johnny Angel didn't fare so well on his ride to disaster, but a lot of singers and songwriters took a long and lucrative ride on C-Am-Dm-G, as shown below.

For a finale, take a shot a *Johnny Angel*.

      C   Am   Dm
Johnny Angel, how I love him. He's got something that I can't resist

  Dm   G7 C
And he doesn't even know that I   exist.

***

Wrapping It Up

Each major chord has a relative minor chord. The relative minors for the I-IV-V chords of a key often make their way into tunes. The relative minor of C is Am, of F is Dm, and of G is Em. Relative minors enable you to play a new range of songs and tunes, including doo-wop.

How is a minor chord constructed? Flat the middle note of the major chord. For example, a C chord is C-E-G, so a Cm is C-E*b*-G. An F chord is F-A-C, so Fm is F-A*b*-and C, and Gm is G-B*b*-D.

Relative Minors

Have a blast, but don't be a blast. Play or sing loudly enough to be heard, but don't break any eardrums!

Play Well With Others

Easy Transposing

Welcome back! You are now a virtuoso in the key of C, at least in three-chord songs with their relative minors. Smoke rises from your instrument as you jam along with your favorite three-chord songs. Then somebody has the nerve to change the key. Thanks a lot!

Why would you transpose keys? Maybe you really want to sing a song, but while you're trying to sound like Julie Andrews, it's coming out like Edith Bunker. If a key is too high or low for your voice, move up or down to a key you can live with. The music may say E-flat, but no key police will swarm down on you should you decide to change.

Why else change keys? Are you playing in A♭? Did you notice that the bass, mandolin, and fiddle players have stopped playing along? If you're feeling lonely, pick a key that's friendlier to people in your musical circle. In the case of A♭, moving a half step either

Play Well With Others

up or down will put you in the friendlier keys of A or G.

Every time you move from one note to the next, it's a half-step. To move from one key to another, just count the number of half-steps from the key you are in to the key you're going to. Then adjust all the chords in the tune the same number of steps.

Let's move from B♭ to C. Note to those who are math challenged: This involves being able to count to two. C is two half-steps or one whole step higher than B♭. (One whole equals 1/2 plus 1/2.) To transpose, simply move every chord in your progression up two half-steps. The progression B♭-F-E♭-Gm-C becomes C-G-F-Am-D.

Feel free to take a look at your keyboard chart when transposing by counting half-steps. All adjacent keys on the keyboard are a half-step apart. Except for E-F and B-C, which don't have black keys to separate them, adjacent white keys are a whole step apart.

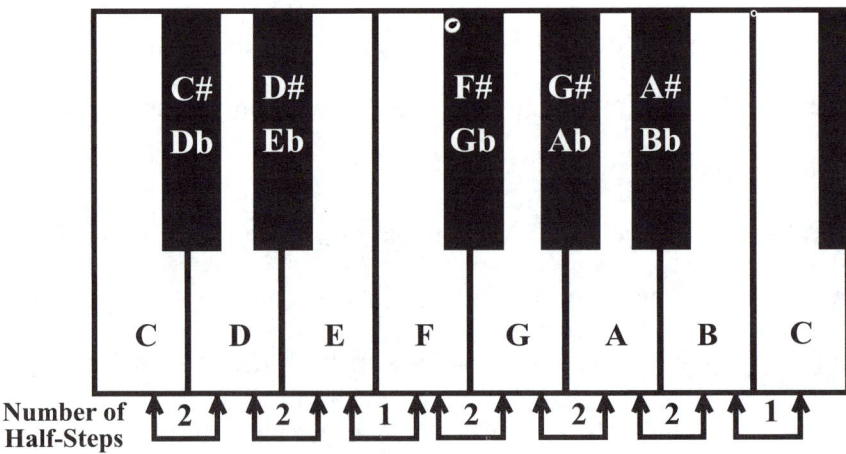

Easy Transposing

***

 <u>What Did We Learn?</u>

Jams are more fun when you play tunes or songs in comfortable keys. To transpose from one key to another, just count the half-steps and shift each chord accordingly.

Mike's Transposing Breakthrough

I remember playing along while someone led *Me and Bobby McGee* at a jam. I'd just learned how to count steps and the leader, who will remain nameless (Martha) had the nerve to change the key from G to A. I counted the steps and for the first time, changing a key in the middle of playing a song didn't reduce me to playing 'air chords.'

Play Well With Others

Capo and Capoese

What if the guitarist plays a song really well in the key of G, but the key of B♭ best fits the singer's voice? A capo, a little clamp that fits over guitar frets, can save the day—or at least make the song better. A capo, used most commonly on guitars or banjos, but also occasionally on a mandolin or other fretted stringed instruments, changes the key of a song without changing the fingerings of the chords played.

To play the guitar in G position while the singing key is really B♭, the guitarist clamps a capo around the neck of the guitar on the third fret, then plays chord configurations of the key of G. You can't strap a capo around a singers' neck, so guitarists, you have to give in.

Here's how it works. A capo holds down all six of the strings of a guitar or banjo across the same fret, and by doing so, shortens each string and raises the pitch of each note. A capo placed on the first fret raises the pitch of each string by a half-step, placed on the

Play Well With Others

second fret raises the pitch by a two half steps (a whole step), placed on the third fret raises the pitch by three half steps, and so forth.

For example, when a capo is placed on the second fret, the G string on a guitar vibrates as an A note and the G chord becomes an A chord—G raised two half steps. Similarly, a C chord becomes a D and D becomes E. Musicians playing non-capoed instruments such as stand-up bass or violin think in A, the *concert key*, the actual key of the song, while the guitarist is thinking and possibly calling out chords in the key of G—the language of *capoese*.

G Chord - capoese   G Chord - capoese
G Chord - concert   A Chord - concert

When some, but not all musicians are playing with a capo, communication between musicians can be tricky. The musicians, in essence, have to transpose between the capoese key and concert key. When translating between the capo key and the concert or actual key, notice two things:

1. The chord *shapes* (what chord it appears that the guitarist, using a capo, is playing) and

2. On what *fret* the capo is placed.

Capo and Capoese

If the guitarist is playing chords in the key of G, with a capo on the 2nd fret, the concert or actual key being played is A, (G moved up two half steps). However, if the guitarist is playing chords in the key of A, with the capo on the second fret, the concert key is B, (A moved up two half steps). If your head hurts from reading this, look at the keyboard diagram. It's a lot easier to see than read about it.

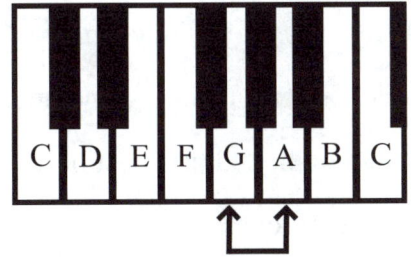 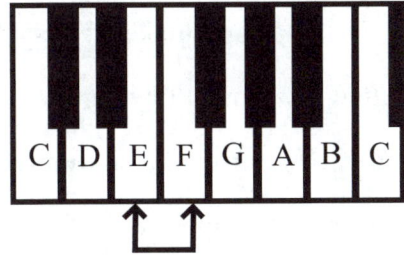

G Capoed up 2 half-steps is A   **E Capoed up a half-step is F**

Let's do a simple translation of capoese chords to concert key for the guitarist backing up the singer in A by playing chords in the key of G. The guitarist tightens a capo around the neck at the second fret, thus moving the key of G up two half steps to A (G→A♭→A).

The guitarist using the capo may call out the chords in the key of G, so non-capoed instrumentalists need to translate the key of G to concert A. A G chord, capoese, is concert A (G moved up two half steps); a C chord, capoese, is a concert D and a D chord capoese is concert E, and any other chord is moved up two half steps. If you are saying, "What the &@#%," then the next sections will give you a simple tool for quickly transposing keys without counting. And remember, this will all begin to make sense when you try it and will make more sense when you practice it.

***

 Wrapping It Up

Using a capo makes it easy to change keys if you're playing a fretted instrument like a guitar or banjo, but musicians playing on non-capoed instruments like fiddle, mandolin, and bass just have to learn to transpose and tough it out on their own.

***

Train Wreck: Playing the wrong chords.

Get Back On Track: Sit out a minute. Watch and listen. Then follow the leader's chord progression. Note whether he or she is using a capo; then note whether *you* are.

A Circle That's Never Unbroken

Is your head swimming in notes and half-steps? Don't worry, we won't let you drown. Counting half-steps is an easy way to transpose keys, as long as the keys are close together. Transposing by counting four or more half-steps is strictly reserved for members of Mensa.

To transpose like an expert, you could enroll at a nearby university and study music theory for a few years. But if you're looking for a quicker way, a Circle of Fifths diagram in your pocket can help you tremendously, especially if you take it out and use it.

What is a fifth and why are fifths in this circle? Notes are a fifth apart when one note is the first note of a major scale (I) and the other note is the fifth (V) of the same scale. By the same token, chords are a fifth apart when their roots are a fifth apart.

When you move clockwise around the Circle of Fifths, the next note is a fifth, or five steps above the note before. Why is this important? Because it opens the door to understanding all kinds

Play Well With Others

of new progressions, and makes transposing a cinch. Amazingly, 12 rotations around the circle covers all the keys and you wind up right where you started, except several octaves higher.

Three-chord songs are particularly easy to transpose this way. Remember the I-IV-V progression? No matter where you go on the circle, if you pick a key, the IV is the chord just before it (counter-clockwise) and the V is the chord just after it (clockwise).

In other words, any three adjacent chords on the circle will be the I-IV-V chords of a key, with the I chord of the key (the tonic) in the middle, the IV chord just before (counter-clockwise), and the V chord just after. So if you are in the key of D, the I-IV-V chords are D, G and A. In E♭ they are E♭, A♭, and B♭.

Circle of Fifths I-IV-V Chords, Sharps, and Flats in Keys

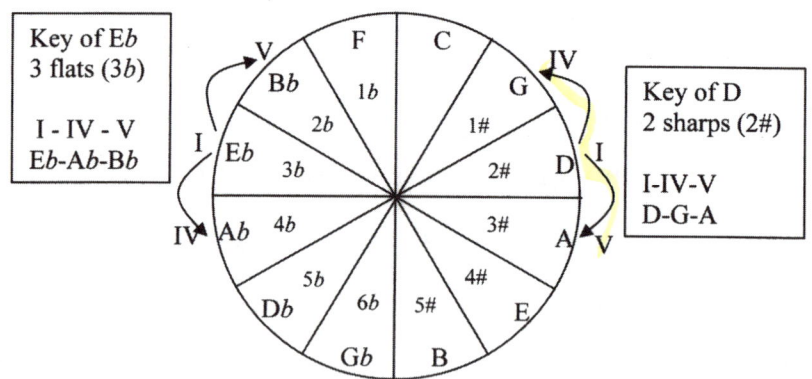

Circle of Fifths

The I's Have It—Transposing Keys by Matching I-IV-V

Here's *Amazing Grace*, first in the Key of C, then in F. Compare this little table to your Circle of Fifths wheel.

Key	I Middle	IV Counterclockwise	V Clockwise
C	C	F	G
F	F	B♭	C

Amazing Grace in C

```
    C                F       C                          G
Amazing Grace, how sweet the sound that saved a wretch like me
    C    C7   F          C              G     C
I once was lost, but now I'm found, was blind, but now I see.
```

Amazing Grace in F

```
    F                Bb      F                          C
Amazing Grace, how sweet the sound that saved a wretch like me
    F    F7   Bb         F              C     F
I once was lost, but now I'm found, was blind, but now I see.
```

Finally, here's *Amazing Grace* in the I-IV-IV format. Some sheet music is printed like this. (We swear it's not an eye chart!)

Play Well With Others

>   I   IV   I   V
> *Amazing Grace, how sweet the sound that saved a wretch like me*
>
>   I   I7   IV   I   V   I
> *I once was lost, but now I'm found, was blind, but now I see.*

Now that you can pick out the I-IV-V chords in any key, you can pick your key for *Amazing Grace*!

***

You Practice: Transpose *Amazing Grace* to at least two keys other than C or F by using the I-IV-V method, and while you're at it, note which key best fits your voice.

***

Easy As Pie Transposing

    It's time to bring out our favorite tool again, the circle of fifths, which looks a lot like a pie chart. Follow along while transposing *Johnny Angel* from the key of C to A. Put together the circle of fifths tool in the back of the book. Rotate the inner wheel so that the A slice on the inside wheel lines up with the C slice on the outside one. Every chord on the outside will line up with the correct chord on the inside. Major chords remain majors, minors remain minors, and 7^{ths} are still 7^{ths}.

    Johnny Angel is shown below in the key of C, then in the key of A.

Circle of Fifths

>   C   Am   Dm
> *Johnny Angel, how I love him. He's got something that I can't resist*
>   Dm   G7   C
> *And he doesn't even know that I..........exist.*

>   A   F#m   Bm
> *Johnny Angel, how I love him. He's got something that I can't resist*
>   Bm   E7   A
> *And he doesn't even know that I..........exist.*

***

You Practice: Transpose *Blue Moon* from the key of C (shown below) to another key by rotating the inner wheel so that the C is paired with the new transposed key of your choice.

>   C Am F   G   C Am F
> *Blue Moon.......... ......you saw me standing alone*
>   G   C Am F   G   C
> *Without a dream in my heart................without a love of my own.*

***

<u>Sharps and Flats in a Key: The Circle Tells All</u>

Do those pesky fiddlers keep asking how many sharps or flats are in the key? The Circle of Fifths comes to the rescue again. When you're moving around the circle, starting with C, every time you

Play Well With Others

move clockwise to the next key there is one more sharp, and when you move counterclockwise there's one more flat. (See diagram at beginning of the section.) Why care? Even if you're not a fiddler, knowing sharps and flats helps you learn scales and instrumental breaks and communicate with other musicians.

Chord Progressions Made Easy on the Circle of Fifths

Let's move on from the I-IV-V thing because there is so much more! Some of the really fun songs take a ride on the circle, jumping clockwise four wedges, then bouncing back counter clockwise, visiting every single chord on the return trip. This is a classic circle of fifths progression in swing, ragtime, bluegrass and other styles of music.

Excited? So are we. Let's demonstrate with the key of C. Start with C, then jump all the way to E, then work your way back counterclockwise to C. That's C-E-A-D-G-C, as shown on the following diagram.

Circle of Fifths

A Circle of Fifths Chord Progression - C-E-A-D-G in the Key of C

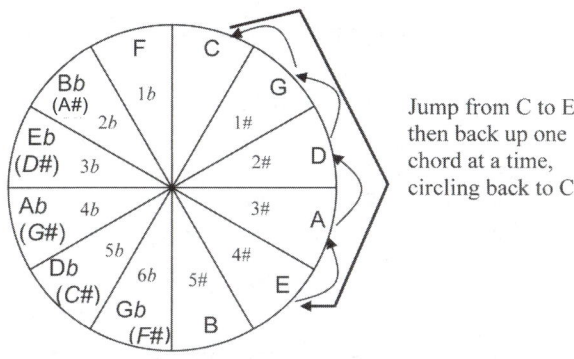

Jump from C to E then back up one chord at a time, circling back to C.

One of the all-time favorite Tin Pan alley songs, *Five Foot Two,* played in C, takes the express route to E (7th), then rides the local back to C, stopping at A, D, and G. To really jazz it up, play all the chords as 7ths, except for C.

C   E7   A7
Five foot two, eyes of blue, but oh what those five feet could do
      D7   G7   C
Has anybody seen my gal?.

Sometimes you run across a shortened circle of fifths progression where you start with the I chord, jump just three steps clockwise, then take the scenic route back to the I. In C that's C-A7-D7-G7-C. This is circle of fifths lite, cutting out one piece of pie (the E). This progression appears in the last line of *Bill Bailey* as shown below in the key of C.

Play Well With Others

>   *F*   *C*   *A7*
> *I know I'm to blame, well, ain't it a shame?*
>   *D7*   *G7*   *C*
> *Bill Bailey won't you please come home?*

***

You Practice: Play the progression C-E-A-D-G-C, a full circle of fifths, and listen to how it sounds. Then play a circle of fifths again, but start with G. That's G-B-E-A-D-G. Now try it with *Five Foot Two* in both keys. Add some sevenths and play the progressions with a swing rhythm and you might have to dance! Now try the Circle of Fifths lite in the key of C. Play a shortened version of the circle, C-A-D-G-C, then in the key of G, G-E-A-D-G. Now play *Bill Bailey* in the keys of C and G.

If you're out of breath, let's take a shorter trip and cut down to three slices of pie. Start with C as the I chord and jump clockwise two chords. That will land you squarely on the D, one whole step above C. Work your way back to C for the common progression C-D-G-C. He*y, Good Lookin,* shown below, and countless other songs use this pattern. Play it and make it hot. Then transpose keys and play it again, Sam!

Circle of Fifths

> C
> *Hey, good lookin. What cha got cookin?*
>
> D7   G7   C
> *How's about cookin up something up with me?*

Diminished 7th Chords

Although many a musician has experienced diminished capacity after a fifth was passed around a circle, diminished 7th chords are something else. Some musicians go through an entire lifetime making beautiful music without ever playing a diminished chord. Diminished 7th chords may even be frowned upon in some circles or genres of music. With that said, however, a diminished 7th chord here and there really adds a delicious character, particularly to some swing or blues songs.

The following version of *Four Leaf Clover* in the key of C goes first from C to D7 (two slices around the circle), has a relative minor to C, a diminished 7th chord, and some ninth chords. (See the "Nuts and Bolts" section for more on diminished sevenths and ninths.)

Play Well With Others

> C   D7
> I'm looking over a four leaf clover, that I overlooked before
>
> G9   C   Am
> One leaf is sunshine, the second is rain,
>
> D7   G9
> Third is the roses that grow in the lane.
>
> C   D7
> No need explaining, the one remaining, is somebody I adore
>
> F9   Adim7   C   Am   F9   G9   C
> I'm looking over a four leaf clover, that I overlooked before

Wrapping It Up

A Circle of Fifths diagram is a tool for picking out relative minors, transposing keys, and identifying common chord progressions. Any three adjacent chords on the circle will be the I, IV, V chords of a key. The I chord will be in the middle, the IV chord counterclockwise, and the V chord clockwise.

Jumping clockwise three or four chords, then working your way back to the I chord gives you very common progressions found in swing, ragtime, bluegrass, and many other styles of music.

Minor Keys

Minor keys are not the keys you use until you're 21, and neither is it a judgement about the importance of a key. Instead, a song in a minor key has a minor chord as the I or tonic chord, and the melody is based on one of two minor scales. We'll talk about the make-up of minor scales in the Nuts and Bolts chapter at the end of the book.

For now it's enough to know that the I-IV-V structure in minor keys is similar to the I-IV-V structure in major keys. For example, in the key of A, the I-IV-V chords are A, D, and E, while in the Key of Am, the I-IV-V chords are Am-Dm-Em or Am-Dm-E (or E7).

Summertime, one of Gershwin's best-known songs, is shown below in the key of Am.

> *Am*
> *Summertime, and the living is easy*
>
> *Dm*   *E7*
> *Fish are jumpin' and the cotton is high*

Play Well With Others

The old folk song *Scarborough Fair* sometimes has a G chord or Em instead of the E7. This song also has other interesting chord combinations.

> Am   G (or Em)   Am
> *Are you going to Scarborough Fair?*
>   C   D   Am
> *Parsley, Sage, Rosemary and Thyme*

Earlier we mentioned that Am is the relative minor for C, and often shows up instead of a C. Well, it works both ways. In minor keys, a major chord may replace its relative minor. For example, in *Scarborough Fair*, G could replace an Em. So, although Am, Dm, Em or E7 are the foundation chords for songs in the key of Am, the chords C, F and G often creep into the mix.

***

 ## Wrapping It Up

Minor keys, like major keys, are often structured around the I-IV-V chords. In a minor key the I and IV chords are usually minor, while the V chord can be minor or major. Major chords and their relative minors are sometimes interchangeable.

What Key Was That?

You've been practicing and you're in the middle of a hot jam. You're keeping up. Good for you! Somebody who hasn't read this book starts a song without calling out the key. But wait! How do you figure out the chords in a key? One way is to learn to read guitar chord fingering. For you ukulele or mandolin players, that means learning to recognize a few chord positions you'll never use on your own instruments. It also involves transposing if the rhythm guitarist is using a capo.

Put your observation skill to work and spot a guitarist who uses simple chords in standard positions on the first few frets. Don't pay attention to the player who plays bar chords that seem to require eight fingers.

Another way is to quietly find individual notes on your instrument that seem to fit. Pay close attention to notes that blend with the last chord of a song, which is most commonly the I chord. Just like *i* before *e*, there are exceptions. If the last chord leaves the song "hanging," the song is usually in a major key and the last chord is probably either the V chord, or the relative minor of the tonic chord.

***

 Wrapping It Up

To figure out the key of a song, learn to follow guitar fingers or pick out notes that blend with the song, especially the last chord or note.

***

Train Wreck: The lead instrumentalist gets lost during a break.
Get Back On Track: Song leader, start humming the tune where you think the tune should be. As soon as you can, come back in singing a chorus or verse.

Take a Break, But Don't Lose Your Noodle.

When someone asks you to take a break, you don't need to excuse yourself and leave the jam. This means they want you to show off your picking or tooting skills (musically speaking). Stick around and play the melody or improvise a complimentary part.

Want to sound like your favorite lead players? Then start the way they likely did, and learn the scales in every key. Our old friends C and G are good for starters.

If You Ain't got the Scales, You Ain't got the Do-Re-Me.

Thanks to *The Sound of Music,* most of us know what Do-Re-Mi sounds like. That song forms the eight notes, I through VIII, that make up a major scale. Start with a C note on a keyboard and then play every white key (no sharps or flats) until you reach the next C and you have a C Scale.

Play Well With Others

***

You Practice: Play a C scale, then an A scale, then try out some other scales. Listen for that Do-Re-Mi melody.

C Scale: C-D-E-F-G-A-B-C

A Scale: A-B-C#-D-E-F#-G#-A

(See the "Nuts and Bolts" section for the rest of the scales)

***

Pickin' Out a Melody.

Once you can play major scales in several keys, start simply and pick out the melody of a three-chord song in one of the keys you practiced. Try *Amazing Grace* in C. Your starting note will be somewhere in the C chord, either C, E, or G. Find the starting note and pick out the melody. Switch to the key of G, for example, where your starting note will be either a G, B, or D.

Trust your ear and resist the urge to look at the written music. Learning to listen and to trust your ear is key to learning to improvise. Try humming the melody when you practice and play the notes you hum.

Picking a Lead

If you will be picking leads while using a capo, lucky you. Just learn the scales around the chord forms you'll be playing. Some great bluegrass guitarists and banjo players operate mostly in C and G and

Take a Break

let the capo do the transposing for other keys. Blues guitarists tend to play in the keys of E, A and D. If you play without a capo, learn all the scales or you will go off your noodle.

What is noodling, by the way? When you're playing in the background and quietly picking single notes along with the music, you're noodling. When you're playing a lead, you're front and center, playing part or all of the form of the song. Fill-ins are mini-lead parts played between phrases that compliment a lead player or singer.

Noodling is a way to work your way up to improvising a lead or filling-in by picking single notes that fit around the chords and melody. If you don't know what key the song is in, ask! Then play notes within the scale of that key.

Are you in a room by yourself with a recording? Play away and let 'er rip! But if you are in a jam, play very softly. After you've practiced and built confidence, continue to play softly most of the time, bumping up the volume at times to compliment the singer or other lead players or to take a lead. Start with simple, repetitive riffs. Feel free to steal from your favorite recordings. Then build up towards playing those eye-poppers.

Noodle all the time and you'll drive everybody in the jam out of their mind. Besides, constant noodling becomes background noise,

Play Well With Others

and you'll never be a star that way. The best musicians sneak in from nowhere and blow away the audience with their finesse and style. Noodle with discretion, and share your noodle!

Once in a session with Chet Atkins, a guitarist said he was having trouble coming up with a good part. Chet said, "Well, you could try the melody." Good lead parts are founded on the melody, so learn to pick out the tune itself, then work on embellishments.

Once again, the key is listening. **Listen harder than you play!** Brilliant solos sound terrible if they don't blend with the song or tune. On the other hand, playing well together can create pure magic. Practice noodling and listening and someday you'll nail that really nice solo.

***

You practice: Play along with the recording of a song. At first, choose simple songs to try, whether they're country, rock 'n' roll, or folk. What key is the song in? You'll figure it out by playing until you find the notes that blend. Remember that the final chord of a song is usually the tonic or I chord of the key.

When a note makes you cringe, keep going until you pick a winner. Later when you're a pro, your mistakes will morph into embellishments. Notes that blend with the tune may be part of the harmony or melody. Some of the best instrumentalists play some of the melody, then improvise with moving parts or harmony.

Take a Break

***

Wrapping it Up

To play instrumentals, start by learning the scales. Then practice picking out the melody of simple three-chord songs. Listen!

***

Don't play songs too advanced for the jam, and don't take fifteen minutes explaining the chord progressions.

Play Well With Others

Other musicians might not ever tell you directly that you're playing inappropriately. Be sensitive to the music around you and adjust. Avoid playing too loud or too fast.

Fakin' the Blues and the Beat Goes On

Is the crowd too happy? Master the following technique and you'll soon have everybody crying in their beer. We're about to show you how to get a bluesy sound in a solo part.

The C scale is just the alphabet, C-D-E-F-G-A-B-C, starting with C, not A. We're going to talk about "flatting" notes. Flatting notes means playing a note one half-step lower than the scale calls for. To play the blues, flat the third note in the scale. In the key of C, for example, slide between E♭ and E. Flatting the fifth and seventh notes helps to make the tune, and your audience cry. So on occasion, play B♭ instead of a B, and a G♭ instead of a G or slither between the note in the scale and its flatted counterpart. If you're playing chords, experiment with changing some of the chords to 7ths (I-IV-V) to (I7-IV7-V7). Make it sultry.

Just because you're playing a bluesy lead or a lot of 7th chords doesn't necessarily mean you're playing the blues. If you want to play the blues, go to the source: blues artists like Koko Taylor or Muddy Waters and do your best to imitate them.

Play Well With Others

<u>Waltzes, Jigs, and 4/4 Time</u>

"And the beat goes on" and sometimes it goes wrong. To stay on beat, it is useful to understand time signatures or how pulses are felt. When a song is in four-four time (has a time signature of 4/4), each measure is broken into four beats. Generally, however, most 4/4 time fiddle tunes, country, swing or folk songs are felt in a two-beat pulse, with the emphasis on the 1st and 3rd beats of the measure (the down beats). Sometimes, the two beat pulse is described as 'Um-Pa, Um-Pa' with the 'Um' on 1st and 3rd beats of the measure and the 'Pa' (the off beats or back beats) on the 2nd and 4th beats.

One line of *Down by the River Side* is shown below with the four beats written above the lyrics. Done in the old-time black gospel style, the singers would generally emphasize the 1st and 3rd beats (the down beats) then clap their hands on the strong off beat pulse (2nd and 4th beats). In many styles rooted in blues, when instruments are added, the bass typically provides strong down beats while guitars or other rhythm instruments can strum quieter down beats followed by strong back beats. Some instruments, such as mandolins, may just chunk out a strong back beat

```
        4      1 2 3  4    1 2 3 4 1 2  3 4    1 2  34
I'm gonna | lay down my | bur -   dens,| down by the | river  side |
```

Fakin' the Blues and the Beat Goes On

When audiences or jammers clap out a rhythm, variance in styles can really conflict. In swing or blues types tunes, the emphasis would typically be on the off beats. When *Down by the River Side* is done in blues gospel style, people would clap on the 2nd and 4th beat of each measure. Done in more of a white folk song style, people would clap on the 1st and 3rd beats of the measure. In contrast, traditional songs, such as *Auld Lang Syne*, from the British Isles tradition are sung with the lilt on the 1st and 3rd beats and not a very strong back beat. Bluegrass style is rhythmically interesting. Bluegrass has strong down beats with an equally strong, almost echoing back beat.

Some times people count off a 4/4 song with "ONE - TWO, a ONE-two-THREE-four" with "ONE-two-THREE-four" said twice as fast. "ONE – TWO" establishes the down beats and "ONE-two-THREE-four" counts out all four beats, emphasizing the two down beats.

Waltzes are played in three-four (3/4) time, with an emphasis on the first of three beats each measure, ONE – two – three, ONE – two – three. Visualize waltzers swaying on a dance floor and rhythmically sway with them. Emphasize the down beat (1st beat) of each measure and play the next two beats (up beats) softer. Sometimes

Play Well With Others

bass players will play a solid 1st beat, skip the 2nd and play the 3rd beat of each measure at about half the volume of the 1st. This gives that nice waltz feel to the music. Guitarists might roll through a chord on the down beat then up-strum the 2nd and 3rd beats almost as a quieter afterthought. Mandolinists might just chunk the 2nd and 3rd beats, but not quite as loudly as the instruments on the down beat.

Jigs are in six-eight (6/8) time. This means each measure has 6 beats (and the eighth note gets one beat—but that is another book). Playing a jig or playing behind a jig on a rhythm instrument can be tricky. The tempo is very fast. Sing YA–da–da, YA–da–da, very quickly, and you hear all six notes of a measure while feeling the two-beat pulse of a jig. You have to be a really experienced guitarist to back up a fiddler and play all 6 beats of a jig while maintaining the pulse and keeping a steady beat up to tempo. Work up to it by strumming only on the 1st and 4th beats (the two-beat pulse) of each measure. The bass player generally plucks only the 1st and 4th beats. The 6 beats are filled in by notes in the melody or by a really good bodhran player

***

Fakin' the Blues and the Beat Goes On

You Practice: Play a C scale, then play it again, flatting the third and the seventh notes. Then make up your own melodies in C and throw in those flatted thirds, fifths, and sevenths. Sometimes hang on to them and other times slide right up to the third, fifth, or seventh. Then try the same thing in other keys.

***

 Wrapping It Up

Flatting the third, fifth, or seventh notes in a scale and sliding around a bit can get the bluesy sound.

***

Train Wreck: Someone is playing a sultry blues song and you're bouncing around like Richard Simmons.

Get Back On Track: Listen and blend in. If the song is beyond your skill level or in a style with which you are unfamiliar, play very softly or just listen.

Play Well With Others

Nuts and Bolts of Chord Composition and Major and Minor Scales—Your Reference Guide

Since you have gotten this far, you have gone beyond what many fine jammers know about music theory. This should be enough to get you started on understanding the basic structure of songs in Western culture. Here are a few quick tips to help you understand the composition of scales and chords.

♪ The I-III-V notes of a major scale make up a **major chord**.

♪ A **minor chord** is formed from a major chord of the same name, by flatting the third (the middle note of the major chord). The minor chord is also the 1st, 3rd, and 5th notes of a minor scale.

♪ When a chord on a song sheet is labeled with what looks like two chords, C/G for example, play a C chord with G as the bass (lowest note).

♪ To create a 7th **chord**, add the flatted 7th note of the major scale to a major chord.

♪ A **major 7th chord** is the major chord plus the 7th note of the

Play Well With Others

major scale.

🎵 To create a **minor 7th** chord, add the 7th note of the natural minor scale to a minor chord.

🎵 To make a **9th chord**, add the 9th note (also the 2nd note) to the 7th chord.

🎵 To form a **diminished 7th chord**, start on any note then add on three more notes, each 3 half steps up from the previous note. Only three combinations of notes make up diminished chords, so any diminished chord has the name of any one of the four notes in the chord.

🎵 A **sixth chord** adds the 6th of the scale to a major chord and is an inversion (same notes arranged differently) of the relative minor seven chord. For example, C6 has the notes C-E-G-A (with C generally played in the bass); Am7, the relative minor to C, has the same notes A-C-E-G, with A generally played as the bass.

The tables below show the composition of different types of chords in every key.

Major Chords, I-III-V notes of a major scale.

Major Chord	I	III	V
C	C	E	G
G	G	B	D
D	D	F#	A
A	A	C#	E
E	E	G#	B
B	B	D#	F#
F#	F#	A#	C#

Nuts and Bolts

Gb	Gb	Bb	Db
Db	Db	F	Ab
Ab	Ab	C	Eb
Eb	Eb	G	Bb
Bb	Bb	D	F
F	F	A	C

Minor Chords: flat the 3rd of a major chord

Cm	C	Eb	G
Gm	G	Bb	D
Dm	D	F	A
Am	A	C	E
Em	E	G	B
Bm	B	D	F#
F#m	F#	A	C#
Gbm	Gb	Bbb (A)	Db
Dbm	Db	Fb (E)	Ab
Abm	Ab	Cb (B)	Eb
Ebm	Eb	Gb	Bb
Bbm	Bb	Db	F
Fm	F	Ab	C

7th chords: Add the flatted 7th to a major chord I-III-V-VIIb

Chord	I	III	V	VIIb
C7	C	E	G	Bb
G7	G	B	D	F
D7	D	F#	A	C
A7	A	C#	E	G
E7	E	G#	B	D
B7	B	D#	F#	A
F#7	F#	A#	C#	E
Gb7	Gb	Bb	Db	Fb
Db7	Db	F	Ab	Cb
Ab7	Ab	C	Eb	Gb
Eb7	Eb	G	Bb	Db
Bb7	Bb	D	F	Ab
F7	F	A	C	Eb

Play Well With Others

Minor 7th chord: Add the 7th of the natural minor scale to the minor chord.

Cm7	C	E♭	G	B♭
Gm7	G	B♭	D	F
Dm7	D	F	A	C
Am7	A	C	E	G
Em7	E	G	B	D
Bm7	B	D	F#	A
F#m7	F#	A	C#	E
G♭m7	G♭	B♭♭ (A)	D♭	F♭
D♭m7	D♭	F♭ (E)	A♭	C♭
A♭m7	A♭	C♭ (B)	E♭	G♭
E♭m7	E♭	G♭	B♭	D♭
B♭m7	B♭	D♭	F	A♭
Fm7	F	A♭	C	E♭

Major 7th: Add the 7th of the major scale to the major chord

Chord	I	III	V	VII♭
Cmaj7	C	E	G	B
Gmaj7	G	B	D	F#
Dmaj7	D	F#	A	C#
Amaj7	A	C#	E	G#
Emaj7	E	G#	B	D#
Bmaj7	B	D#	F#	A#
F#maj7	F#	A#	C#	E# (F)
G♭maj7	G♭	B♭	D♭	F
D♭maj7	D♭	F	A♭	C
A♭maj7	A♭	C	E♭	G
E♭maj7	E♭	G	B♭	D
B♭maj7	B♭	D	F	A
Fmaj7	F	A	C	E

Diminished 7th chords: The diminished 7th chords below are labeled with flats. The flats could be replaced by the equivalent sharps—D# instead of E♭, for example.

Nuts and Bolts

Diminished 7th Chords

Chords				
Cdim, E*b*dim, G*b*dim, Adim	C	E*b* (D#)	G*b* (F#)	A
D*b*dim, Edim, Gdim, B*b*dim	D*b* (C#)	E	G	B*b* (A#)
Ddim, Fdim, A*b*dim, Bdim	D	F	A*b* (G#)	B

Major Scales

A major scale (sung to the tune of do-re-mi-fa-so-la-ti-do) has the same intervals of half and whole steps as the C scale, which is the white notes of a keyboard, starting with C and ending with C. The keyboard diagram below shows a C scale. The I, II, III, IV, V, VI, VII and VIII notes are 2, 2, 1, 2, 2, 2, 1 half steps apart, respectively

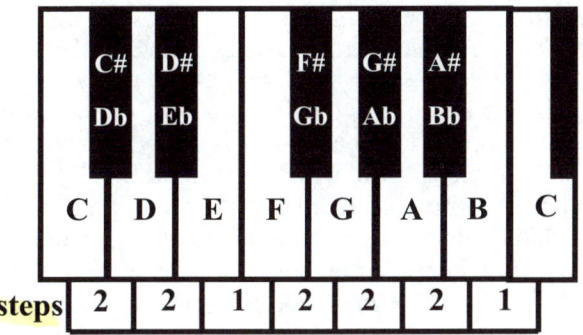

All major scales have the same sequence of half step intervals as the C scale. (Notes are spaced 2, 2, 1, 2, 2, 2 and 1 half steps apart.)

Each major scale is listed in the table below. The highlighted columns are the I-IV-V notes of the scale, the basis for the I-IV-V chords in the key.

Play Well With Others

		I			IV	V		Rel.
Key	No. of sharps or flats	DO I	RE II	MI III	FA IV	SO V	LA VI	TI VII	DO VIII
C	None	C	D	E	F	G	A	B	C
G	1 #	G	A	B	C	D	E	F#	G
D	2 #	D	E	F#	G	A	B	C#	D
A	3 #	A	B	C#	D	E	F#	G#	A
E	4 #	E	F#	G#	A	B	C#	D#	E
B	5 #	B	C#	D#	E	F#	G#	A#	B
F#*	6 #	F#	G#	A#	B	C#	D#	E#	F#
G♭*	6 ♭	G♭	A♭	B♭	C♭	D♭	E♭	F	G♭
D♭	5 ♭	D♭	E♭	F	G♭	A♭	B♭	C	D♭
A♭	4 ♭	A♭	B♭	C	D♭	E♭	F	G	A♭
E♭	3 ♭	E♭	F	G	A♭	B♭	C	D	E♭
B♭	2 ♭	B♭	C	D	E♭	F	G	A	B♭
F	1 ♭	F	G	A	B♭	C	D	E	F

*F# and G♭ are the same key. Each of the notes are the same note. Interesting, in the key of F#, the 7th note is E#. There is no black note between E and F on the keyboard so E# is really an F note. Similarly, the 4th note of the G♭ scale is C♭, which is really a B. The 7th note of the F# scale is called E#, otherwise there would be no representation of E at all in the scale and F would be represented twice. This would make writing music complicated because the music would have to indicate for each F whether it is F (natural) or F#. Odds are, you'll never need to know that, so if it makes no sense to you, unfurrow your brow and move on.

Minor Scales

The natural minor scale that is formed only with white notes on the keyboard (shown below) starts with A (the 6th note of the C scale) and ends with A. As such, an A-minor scale, shown on the diagram, has no sharps or flats (none)—the same as the C scale.

The natural A-minor scale: A-B-C-D-E-F-G-A

Nuts and Bolts

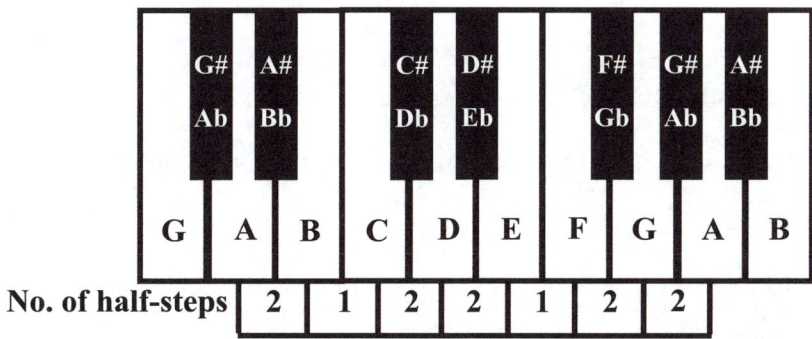

A harmonic minor scale differs by one note from the natural minor scale (of the same key). The 7th note of the natural minor scale is a half step higher on the harmonic scale. In the harmonic A-minor scale, the 7th note is G# rather than G.

Natural A-minor scale and number of half steps between notes:

A B C D E F G A

 2 1 2 2 1 2 2

Harmonic A-minor scale and number of half steps between notes:

A B C D E F G# A

 2 1 2 2 1 3 1

Some songs in the key of A-minor have Em or G chords. Those songs are based on the natural A-minor scale because G is a note in Em and G chords. However, songs in the key of A-minor that have an E chord instead of Em or G are structured around the harmonic A-minor scale because G# is a note in the E chord. Here's another twist. Some tunes alternate within the tune between the two minor scales.

Play Well With Others

Progressions

Learn these progressions and you'll be able play dozens of songs like a pro:

1950s Progression (songs like *Earth Angel, Sha-boom*)

Key	I	VI	IV	V
F major	F	Dm	B♭	C
G major	G	Em	C	D
A major	A	F#m	D	E
B♭ major	B♭	Gm	E♭	F
C major	C	Am	F	G
D major	D	Bm	G	A
E major	E	C#m	A	B

1950s Ballads (*songs like Blue Moon*)

Key	I	VI	II	V
F major	F	Dm	Gm	C
G major	G	Em	Am	D
A major	A	F#m	Bm	E
B♭ major	B♭	Gm	C♭m	F
C major	C	Am	Dm	G
D major	D	Bm	Em	A
E major	E	C#m	F#m	B

Blues (songs like *St. James Infirmary*)

Key	I	IV	V7
D Minor	Dm	Gm	A7
E Minor	Em	Am	B7
F# Minor	F#m	Bm	C#7
G minor	Gm	Cmin	D7
A minor	Am	Dmin	E7
B minor	Bm	Em	F#7
C# minor	C#m	F#m	G#7

Nuts and Bolts

Swing (songs like *I've Got Rhythm*)

Key	I	VI7	II7	V7
F major	F	D7	G7	C7
G major	G	E7	A7	D7
A major	A	F#7	B7	E7
B♭ major	B♭	G7	C7	F7
C major	C	A7	D7	G7
D major	D	B7	E7	A7
E major	E	C#7	F#7	B7

***

Jam Buster Testimonial
"I used to clear the room when I walked in, but after I learned how to play well with others, people even invite me to jams!"—Jack, the ex-jam buster

About The Authors:

Martha Haehl

Martha can't remember a time when she wasn't singing—starting at an early age to harmonize with her sister and making up tunes on the piano. In her adult life, Martha, torn between becoming a math professor or a musician, ultimately decided to do both. Martha plays multiple instruments (11 at last count) and is a song writer and marathon jammer. In her many years as a musician, she's played with numerous groups from acoustic to rock 'n' roll. While a member of *Rosy's Bar and Grill*, Martha performed on Garrison Keillor's *Prairie Home Companion* radio program. Martha is now in a group appropriately called *Checkered Past*. (www.checkeredpastmusic.com) She has also written and published mathematics materials.

Mike Walker

Mike is an award winning writer and publisher who freelanced for magazines and served for seven years as an editor for The Pitch, a weekly paper in Kansas City. Mike is also the author of two books, *Cinemental Journeys,* and *Autos to Airwaves, Mantle to the Mob.* In 2002 Mike acted on a lifelong dream and purchased his first ukulele and he's been addicted ever since. Mike especially loves Tin Pan Alley and the blues. Mike and Martha met at a Kansas City weekly potluck dinner where friends gather, dine, then retire to the living room to make music.

****

By now you should know enough to have all kinds of fun playing with others. If you have any questions, comments, or suggestions, we want to hear them. Please contact us at:

www.hhtmp.com or

info@moonbookstore.com

Play Well With Others

Here's a kit for making your own Circle of Fifths wheel! Just cut the larger wheel out, then the smaller one. Then place the smaller wheel centered on top of the large wheel. Place a pin or brad in the centers of the wheel so you can spin the inner wheel. Laminating before you put them together will make them last a lot longer.

How To Use: If you're playing in the key of C and want to switch to G, make note of all the chords you are using in C. Now turn the inner wheel so that the G lines up with the C on the large wheel. All the chords in the key of C on the large wheel will line up with the new chords used in the key of G on the small wheel.

Also note that just to the right of every key, in smaller print, is the relative minor for that key.

If you'd like to order a more professional wheel with added features, we have them available at: www.hhtmp.com.

Thank you and have fun!

Circle of Fifths Tool

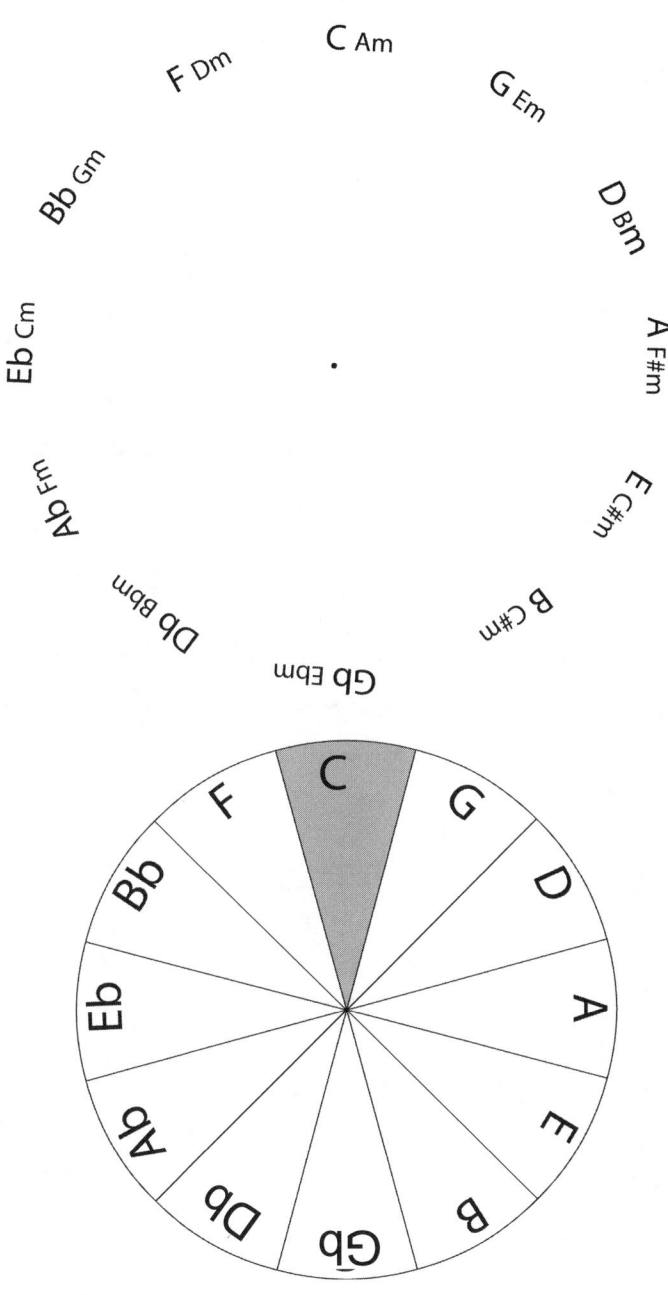

Permissions

BLUE MOON
Music by RICHARD RODGERS Lyrics by LORENZ HART
© 1934 (Renewed) METRO-GOLDWYN-MAYER INC. All Rights Controlled by EMI ROBBINS CATALOG INC. (Publishing) and ALFRED PUBLISHING CO., INC. (Print)
All Rights Reserved   Used by Permission of ALFRED PUBLISHING CO., INC.

FIVE FOOT TWO, EYES OF BLUE
Lyrics by SAM LEWIS and JOE YOUNG Music by RAY HENDERSON
© 1925 (Renewed) EMI FEIST CATALOG INC. Rights for the Extended Renewal Term in the U.S. Controlled by RAY HENDERSON MUSIC COMPANY, EMI FEIST CATALOG INC. and WAROCK MUSIC CORP. Rights outside the U.S. Controlled by EMI FEIST CATALOG INC. (Publishing)
and ALFRED PUBLISHING CO., INC. (Print)
All Rights Reserved   Used by Permission of ALFRED PUBLISHING CO., INC., HAL LEONARD, INC, and HENDERSON MUSIC CO.

DOIN' TIME
Words and Music by GEORGE GERSHWIN, IRA GERSHWIN
and DUBOSE AND DOROTHY HEYWARD
© DUBOSE AND DOROTHY HEYWARD MEMORIAL FUND PUBLISHING., IRA GERSHWIN MUSIC, GEORGE GERSHWIN MUSIC, LOU DOG PUBLISHING and MARSHALL ARTS MUSIC All Rights on behalf of DUBOSE AND DOROTHY HEYWARD MEMORIAL FUND PUB., IRA GERSHWIN MUSIC and GEORGE GERSHWIN MUSIC Administered by WB MUSIC CORP. All Rights Reserved {Contains Samples from "SUMMERTIME" from PORGY AND BESS by GEORGE GERSHWIN, DUBOSE & DOROTHY HEYWARD and IRA GERSHWIN. © GEORGE GERSHWIN MUSIC, IRA GERSHWIN MUSIC, DUBOSE AND DOROTHY HEYWARD MEMORIAL FUND PUBLISHING. All Rights Administered by WB MUSIC CORP.} {Contains Samples from "FIGHT FOR THE RIGHT" by RICK RUBIN, ADAM YAUCH, ADAM HOROVITZ. © WB MUSIC CORP., AMERICAN DEF TUNES, INC., BROOKLYN DUST MUSIC. All Rights on behalf of AMERICAN DEF TUNES Administered by WB MUSIC CORP.}
All Rights Reserved   Used by Permission of ALFRED PUBLISHING and HAL LEONARD, INC.

I'M LOOKING OVER A FOUR LEAF CLOVER
Lyrics by MORT DIXON Music by HARRY WOODS
© 1927 (Renewed) WARNER BROS. INC. Rights for the Extended Renewal Term in the U.S. Controlled by CALLICOON MUSIC (c/o The Songwriters Guild Of America) and OLDE CLOVER LEAF MUSIC (c/o Fred Ahlert Music Corp. / Bug Music, Inc.) Canadian Rights Controlled by WB MUSIC CORP.
All Rights Reserved   Used by Permission of ALFRED PUBLISHING CO., INC. and CALLICOON MUSIC.

JOHNNY ANGEL
Words by LYN DUDDY Music by LEE POCKRISS
© 1962 (Renewed) EMILY MUSIC COMPANY and IVANHOE MUS
All Rights Reserved   Used by Permission of ALFRED PUBLISHING CO., INC.

HEY, GOOD LOOKIN'
Words and Music by Hank Williams
Copyright © 1951 Sony/ATV Music Publishing LLc and Hiriam Music in the U.S.A
Copyright Renewed
This arrangement Copyright © 20008 Sony/ATV Music Publishing LLC and Hiriam Music in the U.S.A
All rights on behalf of Hiram MNusic Administred by Rightsong Music, Inc.
All Rights outside the U.S.A. Controlled by Sony/ATV Music Publishing LLC
All Rights on behalf of Sony/ATV Music Publishing LLC Administered by Sony/ATV Music Publishing LLC, 8 Music Square West, Nashville, TN 37203
International Copyright Secured All Rights Reserved. Used by Permission of HAL LEONARD, INC.

*****

The authors also wish to thank Gary Tannen and Lynn Synder for their help in designing the circle of fifths.